First published in hardcover in the United States of America in 1998 by
Thames and Hudson Inc., 500 Fifth Avenue, New York, New York 10110

First published in Great Britain in 1998 by Thames and Hudson Ltd, London

Library of Congress Catalog Card Number 98-60187

ISBN 0–500–54221–X

British Library Cataloguing-in-Publication data
A catalogue record for this book is available from the British Library

Designed by Liz Trovato

Map by Jack Scott

Printed and bound in Hong Kong

MANHATTAN SHORES

An Expedition Around the Island's Edge

BY LAURA ROSEN

THAMES AND HUDSON

For Adrian

ACKNOWLEDGMENTS

I wish to thank the many people who have shown me unfamiliar waterfront territories, provided access, protected me in a few unsavory locations, given me historical and technical information, checked for blunders and were there to bounce ideas when I got stuck.

Arne Abramowitz, Cy A Adler, Sorab Bakhshi, Mary Barber, Peter Basich, Marc Boddewyn, Veselko Buntic, Bill Chassé, Kenneth Cobb, Dennis Crowe, Nestor Danyluk, Peter Derrick, Noreen Doyle, Mary Lee Duff, Bruce Einsohn, Charlotte Fahn, Ann Foker, Tom Fox, Rob Friedman, Brian Gerber, Mindy Giberstone, Stan Greenberg, René Hanau, Hedy Hartman, Clare Hayden, Isabel Hill, Bill Hine, Tessa Huxley, Peter King, John Kriskiewicz, Jonathan Kuhn, Floyd Lapp, Gordon Linzner, Theresa Llorente, Ira Mandelbaum, Glenn Mann, Bob Marshall, Vincent McGowan, Charles McKinney, Marc Miller, Michelle Moore, Beth O'Leary, Robert A. Olmsted, Robert M. Paley, Brenda Parnes, Carol A. Pieper, Robert Politzer, Nicholas Quennell, Naima Rauam, Marcia Reiss, Andy Rosina, Peter Rothschild, Carla Rupp, Penny Ryan, Charles Sachs, Jane Schachat, David Sirkin, Selvin T. Southwell, Lawrence Stelter, Gary Stilovich, Joseph Strein and Hsienhua Tan, Shorewalkers, Bob Walker, Kevin Wolfe, Andrew Wong, Wilbur Woods, and Devra Zetlan.

Special thanks also to Chuck Kelton at Kelton Labs NYC.

I especially want to thank Adrian Spratt for his guidance and emotional support during the entire course of this project. I also want to thank my parents and Adrian's parents for their advice, patience and encouragement.

CONTENTS

INTRODUCTION

I have spent a good part of my adult life photographing Manhattan's interior regions as an architectural photographer. In 1994, I decided to explore the island's edges and to photograph the experience of traveling through all of Manhattan's varied waterfront areas. A journey around Manhattan is a journey in time as well as geography since so much of New York's history is evident on its waterfront. As I imagine it would be for anyone who grew up in or near New York City, mine was a journey in personal history too.

When I was a child in the 1950s, I would travel to Manhattan with my parents from our town in New Jersey. As we crossed the George Washington Bridge we admired the Hudson River and the cliffs of the Palisades stretching north on the New Jersey side. Looking south, we saw the sweep of Manhattan and the familiar profiles of its skyscrapers in midtown and downtown. As we traveled south on the Henry Hudson Parkway, the river was very close, just beyond the ragged greenery at the water's edge, and its hue could change from hazy silver to blue or brown. Then we were on the elevated West Side Highway (which my father told us was officially called the Miller Highway) passing over the railyards that extended from 72nd Street to 59th Street. From this high vantage point we could see if any huge funnels were visible above the ocean liner piers off the West 40s and 50s. It was exciting to glimpse the big ships between the dark and decaying pier sheds as we drove by. We would identify them: the *United States,* the *France,* the *Queen Mary,* the *Stockholm,* the *Andrea Doria.* Their blade-sharp prows that flared out at the top were both fascinating and scary. The

television image of the sinking *Andrea Doria,* on its side in the ocean after it collided with the *Stockholm* in July 1956, was both terrifying and unsettling in its miniature scale.

Sometimes we traveled on West Street or on the southern ends of 11th or 12th Avenue, beneath the elevated highway. The car vibrated loudly as it went over the granite-block pavement. The underside of the roadway above us was black, and the once-ornate facades of the piers created a shadowy wall between us and the river. People said what a shame it was that the waterfront was the first thing you saw when you came to New York by ship. The waterfront seemed to be a place that you just didn't go to unless you were a ship passenger or a longshoreman.

Occasionally we drove down the East Side on the Harlem River Drive. From the ramps leading to the drive at 178th Street, we would see the High Bridge Tower rising above Highbridge Park's forested cliffs, like a scene from a Hudson River School painting, but it faced the refuse-strewn Harlem River shoreline. Farther south, new rows of housing projects faced the industrial shoreline's progression of old steel bridges. When the highway disappeared into a tunnel at 92nd Street, it meant we were approaching our midtown destination and would soon turn away from the water.

This was the era of bright, optimistic modernism. The George Washington Bridge, completed in 1931, had been the first automobile-age bridge to Manhattan and its silvery skeleton still symbolized the Modern. White concrete interstate highways were beginning to connect America and glass skyscrapers were rising above the dark clutter of earlier times. Sometimes we would visit the Museum of Modern Art, which had a cool pale gray exterior and a silvery curved canopy over its entrance. The roof over the museum's terrace restaurant had a row of circles cut out of it that caused spotlights of sun to move slowly around us. On Park Avenue, the smooth, glassy surface of the Lever Brothers headquarters stood in contrast with all the complicated masonry of the buildings around it. The slab of the United Nations Secretariat, resplendent on a white platform, had only recently replaced the slaughterhouses on the East Side waterfront.

As a child I had a fantasy of a huge shovel scraping away all the dark old-fashioned clutter to make room for light, air and brilliant modern surfaces. For better or worse, the gleaming jet airplane and efficient container ships did just that to Manhattan's commercial waterfront.

By the mid-1960's, highways encircled most of Manhattan island. Some were elevated to carry traffic over railyards and loading areas for piers, others were hidden in tunnels or built through parks. At the same time, shipping was leaving Manhattan's docks for the more spacious and efficient container ports in New Jersey and Brooklyn. Jet service to Europe began in 1958, and ocean liners were soon replaced by airplanes for international travel. The departure of port activities left a large vacuum by the 1970's. Since that time, developers, community groups, politicians and environmentalists have all been attempting to shape the waterfront to their visions of its future. By the early 1990's, the elevated West Side Highway was demolished south of 59th Street

and the wall of pier sheds and decaying industrial structures around much of the southern portion of Manhattan's waterfront had almost entirely disappeared, revealing that Manhattan is, in fact, an island with a view.

My photographic journey around Manhattan's edge consisted of many individual expeditions and return visits, during which I explored and photographed specific sections of the waterfront. Most often I went alone or, occasionally, with a friend. A few times I joined the Shorewalkers, a nonprofit environmental organization that explores the shores and wetlands in the New York City area and holds an annual hike called the "Great Saunter" around Manhattan's entire shoreline each May.

I have organized this book as a clockwise journey, starting just north of the George Washington Bridge, so that the more familiar southern parts of the waterfront are in the middle of the progression and seen in the context of the whole, which is about 32 miles long. The book is divided into 10 regions. The distances in each region vary and the camera is not always pointed in the clockwise direction. I traveled light and used very simple camera equipment. Many of the photographs were taken with the old twin lens Rolleiflex that my grandfather, who took the picture of me and my parents on the facing page, bought in 1954. Images glow on the ground glass screen on its top, protected by the shadows of the folding black walls that come up its edges. After each shot, it was necessary to turn the crank on the side of the camera clockwise and then counterclockwise to advance the film for the next shot, a motion that imitated my epicyclic progress around the island.

CHAPTER ONE

MANHATTAN'S NORTHWESTERN TIP

I once lived in a small apartment on Riverside Drive in Washington Heights that had a terrace with a view of the Hudson River. This journey around Manhattan begins near that place, just north of the George Washington Bridge, in Fort Washington Park. The park, at the edge of the Hudson between 158th Street and Dyckman Street, was acquired by the City in stages between 1896 and 1927. Its shoreline is remote and difficult to reach because of railroad tracks and the Henry Hudson Parkway that both run through the park's entire length. Tracks were first laid here by the Hudson River Railroad in the late 1840's, long before the park's creation, and are now used for Amtrak passenger service. The Henry Hudson Parkway came through here in 1936. North of the George Washington Bridge, the park is most easily reached by walking south from an entrance on Dyckman Street, which means that this clockwise journey begins with a hairpin turn.

Fort Tryon Park is on the steep hills just upland from Fort Washington Park between 190th Street and the end of Riverside Drive at Dyckman Street. Fort Washington was the name of the series of fortifications in the area that were Manhattan's last to fall to the British during the American Revolution. The British occupiers renamed the part of the fortifications where Fort Tryon Park is today after Sir William Tryon, the last British colonial governor of New York and major general of the Provincial Forces of the Crown during the Revolution. Fort Tryon Park, on the site of former country estates that replaced the Revolutionary fortifications in the 19th century, was designed by Olmsted Brothers and dedicated in 1936. At around the same time, medieval cloisters were brought to the park from Europe and incorporated into The Cloisters museum, designed by Charles Collens and completed in 1938 as a branch of the Metropolitan Museum, specializing in medieval art. The 67-acre park and The Cloisters were gifts to New York City from John D. Rockefeller, Jr. To protect the park's view across the Hudson, Rockefeller bought land on top of the Palisades, the rocky cliffs on the river's western bank, for Palisades Interstate Park.

Inwood Hill Park, which covers the west side of Manhattan north of Dyckman Street, was acquired by the City in stages between 1916 and 1941. Dyckman Fields, the flat section of ball fields along the Hudson, was created with landfill in the 1930's in exchange for land taken from the park when the Henry Hudson

Parkway was cut through it. A footbridge crosses over the railroad tracks that separate Dyckman Fields from the rest of Inwood Hill Park, which is the location of Manhattan's only natural forest. The name Dyckman is from the family of Jan Dyckman, a 17th-century settler whose descendants remained in the area until the early 20th century.

Inwood Hill Park's northern shoreline is now separated from the Bronx by the United States Ship Canal, but when Henry Hudson anchored the *Half Moon* nearby in 1609, a small creek separated Manhattan's northern tip from the Bronx. Early Dutch settlers called the creek Spuyten Duyvil, variously said to mean "spite of the devil," "spouting devil" and "spouting spring in the meadow." After the Erie Canal connected the Great Lakes to the Hudson at Albany in 1825, a canal was proposed to go around the northern tip of Manhattan to allow ships coming down the Hudson to reach the Harlem and East Rivers and Long Island Sound without going around its southern tip. Construction of the federally funded canal between the Hudson and Harlem Rivers began in 1888, after decades of false starts and alternate proposals, including one to fill in the Harlem River to make Manhattan a peninsula. The United States Ship Canal, often called the Harlem Ship Canal, became navigable in 1895, but it wasn't until 1938 that the canal and the Harlem River were sufficiently dredged and straightened for deep-water ships. Today, it is rare that anything larger than a sightseeing boat passes through the canal, which is generally perceived as part of the Harlem River.

The railroad bridge and the Henry Hudson Bridge between Inwood Hill Park and Riverdale, in the Bronx, were built to accommodate the Ship Canal. The railroad bridge, which replaced an earlier one in 1900, has a swing span that rotates on a central column to create an opening for boats, which it must do several times a day because the bridge's clearance at high tide can be as little as five feet. The Henry Hudson Bridge, which opened as part of the Henry Hudson Parkway in 1936, has an 840-foot-long arch and 142 1/2-foot clearance, making a movable span unnecessary.

Between the park and Broadway, the shoreline is on private property belonging to Columbia University and closed to the public. From here it is necessary to detour upland to reach the industrial shoreline east of the Broadway Bridge.

Fort Washington Park at about 190th Street. The Palisades on the New Jersey side of the Hudson are to the left.

View of Fort Tryon Park, looking south from the tower of The Cloisters. Fort Washington Park, at the water's edge, is hidden except for Jeffrey's Hook, the small point of land where the George Washington Bridge's Manhattan tower stands. **10**

11   The Linden Terrace lookout in Fort Tryon Park is on the site where Fort Tryon stood during the Revolutionary War.

Above Fort Tryon Park's treetops, the tower of The Cloisters is visible from the marina at the end of Dyckman Street.
Below, an Amtrak train passes under a support structure for the Henry Hudson Parkway.

Under a lease from the Parks Department, a private operator runs the marina and fishing pier at the end of Dyckman Street.

The fishing pier at the end of Dyckman Street. The Hudson River begins in the Adirondacks 315 miles north of the city.
An estuary of the Atlantic, the river is tidal for 154 miles and saline for 60 miles.

Inwood Hill Park's hills, the site of Manhattan's only natural forest, are behind the picnickers and soccer players at Dyckman Fields.
Bronx apartment buildings are visible in the distance.

The swing railroad bridge in its open position, seen from a boat that has just passed through the United States Ship Canal.
The Henry Hudson Bridge is beyond the railroad bridge. **16**

The Henry Hudson Bridge from Inwood Hill Park's Ship Canal shoreline at low tide. The New Jersey Palisades are visible beyond Riverdale in the
Bronx, below the bridge's arch. Metro-North's Spuyten Duyvil railroad station is on the Riverdale shoreline.

The tide coming in near Columbia University's boat house. The tall light poles are at Baker Field, the university's sports complex. **18**

The cliff on the Bronx shoreline was created when the ship canal was straightened by cutting through a Bronx peninsula.

The "C" is for Columbia University.

CHAPTER TWO

THE UPPER HARLEM RIVER

The United States Ship Canal meets the Harlem River (not really a river but a tidal strait between Manhattan and the Bronx) near the Broadway Bridge. All of the bridges on the Ship Canal and the Harlem River were designed with high arches or movable spans to allow for ships traveling between the Hudson and East Rivers. The Broadway Bridge has a vertical lift span that rises between two towers while remaining parallel to the water. The bridge, sometimes called the Ship Canal Bridge, began carrying traffic, pedestrians and the IRT West Side local subway lines in 1962. It replaced a 1907 swing bridge which, in turn, replaced an 1895 swing bridge that was too small to carry the subway line that had just reached northern Manhattan. The center span of the 1895 bridge was floated to 207th Street in 1908 to become the swing span on the University Heights Bridge, where it remains today. The 1907 Broadway Bridge was then scrapped.

In one small area, the Borough of Manhattan extends to the other side of the Ship Canal. The community of Marble Hill, on the north side of the Broadway Bridge, had been the northernmost tip of Manhattan island before the canal was cut through its southern edge. When the Spuyten Duyvil Creek on Marble Hill's northern edge was filled in, the community became attached to the Bronx but has technically remained part of Manhattan.

The Harlem River shoreline between the Broadway Bridge and Dyckman Street is occupied by a large subway yard, a bus yard, a sanitation repair facility, a Con Edison facility, a supermarket and several small businesses. The water's edge is generally inaccessible except at the ends of desolate, garbage-strewn streets. My favorite way to see this part of the river is from the walkway of the University Heights Bridge.

At the eastern end of Dyckman Street is a small cove named Sherman Creek, a remnant of a creek that once went halfway across the island. The cove's northern edge, reachable from Academy Street, is littered with old tires, car parts and other refuse. Three small private boat clubs remain alongside decaying boats from abandoned boat clubs on the cove's southern end, which is reachable by a service road behind P.S. 5, an elementary school that was built at the end of Dyckman Street in 1993.

Highbridge Park is on the forested cliffs overlooking the Harlem River between Dyckman Street and 155th Street. An esplanade at the water's edge passes under the arches of the Washington, Alexander Hamilton and High Bridges, which rise from the foot of the park's cliffs and soar over the river. The Washington Bridge, at 181st Street, first opened for travelers in 1888. The Alexander Hamilton Bridge, at 178th Street, was completed in 1963 as part of Interstate 95 between the George Washington Bridge and the Cross Bronx Expressway. The 1848 High Bridge, at 174th Street, was a Croton Water System aqueduct with a walkway on top and is the oldest extant bridge to Manhattan. In 1927, five of the bridge's 15 original arches were replaced by a single steel arch to accommodate Ship Canal traffic. Today, its walkway is closed and it has not carried water for decades.

The esplanade at the base of the cliffs of Highbridge Park runs between the river and the Harlem River Driveway. The Driveway, not to be confused with the Harlem River Drive to the south, was called the Harlem River Speedway when it opened in 1898 as a drive for the then fashionable high-speed horse-drawn vehicles of the wealthy. Crowds came to see the spectacle on the Speedway when it was new, but now this area is so desolate that it is best to bring plenty of company when exploring it. My first visit was with the Shorewalkers on their annual "Great Saunter" hike around Manhattan's entire shoreline. We kept on the esplanade until we reached a traffic ramp at about 165th Street, which we walked up, without the benefit of a sidewalk, and then continued south along Edgecombe Avenue to 145th Street. The detour was necessary because the waterfront is blocked between 165th Street and 145th Street by the Harlem River Drive and private parking lots.

A No. 1 IRT subway train crossing the Broadway Bridge.

The 207th Street Subway Yard covers the waterfront between 215th and 208th Streets. The University Heights Bridge at 207th Street is to the left. The tall buildings at center are River Park Towers in the Bronx.

The University Heights Bridge leads to West Fordham Road in the South Bronx. Its 24-foot clearance, the minimum standard for bridges on the Harlem River, allows tourist boats to pass under it when it is closed.

From the University Heights Bridge's walkway, a partially demolished Con Edison plant near
Dyckman Street is visible in front of the hills of Highbridge Park. **24**

View south from the northern edge of Sherman Creek. An egret, at center, wades among rotting boats at abandoned boat clubs.
A duck and ducklings are little more than specks to the far right. The upper stories of P.S. 5 are visible to the right, and the tops of
River Park Towers in the Bronx are over the trees at center.

View of High Bridge and High Bridge Tower from the Bronx. The tower, built in 1872, once contained a huge water tank that stabilized the pressure of the water carried by the High Bridge.

The arches of the Washington, Alexander Hamilton and High Bridges cross above an esplanade that was once part of the Harlem River Speedway.

Looking northeast from High Bridge Tower, the Harlem River Driveway and the esplanade are at the water's edge.
The ramp winding through Highbridge Park connects the Harlem River Driveway with Interstate 95. At center are the Alexander
Hamilton Bridge and the double-arched Washington Bridge. The University Heights Bridge is in the distance.

Looking southeast from the tower, the Harlem River Driveway hugs the shoreline, which becomes inaccessible by foot south of the curving overpass ramp at the far right, near 165th Street. South of the ramp, the waterfront roadway is called the Harlem River Drive. Macombs Dam Bridge, at 155th Street, is the first bridge in the distance.

CHAPTER THREE

A landowner named Robert Macomb built a combined toll bridge and dam across the Harlem River near 155th Street in 1813, turning the upper Harlem River into his own mill pond. His neighbors, fed up with the tolls and the obstruction to navigation, tore the bridge down in 1838. The bridge now at this site, built in 1895, swings open for ships and is free to cross, but still carries the name Macombs Dam Bridge.

In the 1880's, before the Harlem River was transformed from a popular scenic location to a commercial waterway, boat houses and rowing clubs dotted the irregular shoreline between 149th and 159th Streets and pleasure boats crowded the river in good weather. The few boat houses that remained at the turn of the century shared the waterfront with commercial buildings, coal yards, and railyards for the 6th and 9th Avenue Elevated Railroads. The Polo Grounds, which overlooked the Harlem River at 157th Street, was the home of the New York Giants baseball team between 1891 and 1957 and various other teams including the football Giants, the Yankees and the Mets, before it was demolished in 1964. Apartment towers have replaced the Polo Grounds and its neighboring railyards. The Harlem River Drive, which replaced industrial waterfront structures south of the 165th Street traffic ramp in the 1960's, has no esplanade.

There are eight bridges with spans that either rotate or lift for ships to pass between 155th Street and 103rd Street. The Macombs Dam Bridge at 155th Street (1895), the 145th Street Bridge (1905), the Madison Avenue Bridge (1910), the Third Avenue Bridge (1899) and the Willis Avenue Bridge (1901) are swing bridges of similar design with spans that open by rotating on pedestals. Metro-North's railroad bridge at Park Avenue (1954), the Triborough Bridge's lift span at 125th Street (1936) and the pedestrian bridge to Ward's Island at 103rd Street (1951)

MACOMBS DAM BRIDGE TO EAST 90TH STREET

have vertical lift spans. With the exception of the railroad bridge, each of these bridges has a walkway.

A walkway over the Harlem River Drive at 142nd Street leads to Harlem Beach, a narrow strip of undeveloped City parkland at the water's edge between 145th Street and the Third Avenue Bridge. It is one of the rare grassy spots on Manhattan's waterfront without a railing and there always seem to be people fishing here. Local community groups and the City plan to transform it into a landscaped esplanade and recreation area. South of the Third Avenue Bridge, an abandoned concrete plant and mountains of asphalt stand at the water's edge. Another mountain, this one of salt, sits between the Willis Avenue Bridge and the Triborough Bridge, stored there by the Department of Sanitation for spreading on icy roads in the winter.

The waterfront highway between the Triborough Bridge and the Battery was named the Franklin D. Roosevelt Drive shortly after World War II but New Yorkers almost always refer to it as the FDR Drive, or sometimes by its original name, the East River Drive. An esplanade between the water and the FDR Drive begins just south of the Triborough Bridge and continues to Carl Schurz Park at 92nd Street. Along its course are a recreational pier at 107th Street and the pedestrian bridge to Ward's Island at 103rd Street. Ward's Island and Randall's Island, connected to each other with landfill, have large areas of parkland surrounding several hospitals, municipal facilities and viaducts for the Triborough Bridge and the New York Connecting Railroad (Hell Gate) Bridge, now used by Amtrak. Hell Gate is the name of the turbulent waters around Ward's Island where the Harlem River meets the East River. At 90th Street, the esplanade runs into Carl Schurz Park as the FDR Drive tunnels under the park.

View southwest from the Macombs Dam Bridge at 155th Street. The barges and cranes are for the construction of the Oak Point Link, a freight rail line on the Bronx shoreline, at left, that will run on a trestle to connect railyards in the South Bronx. The Harlem River Drive is visible on the far shoreline.

Waves from a Circle Line boat roll toward the Shorewalkers as they proceed on a narrow section of Harlem Beach during their annual "Great Saunter" hike around Manhattan's entire waterfront. The 145th Street Bridge behind them is typical of the swing bridges on the Harlem River.

The walkway on the Madison Avenue Bridge. The white tarpaulins collect lead paint residue that is vacuumed away through the flexible pipes during abrasive blasting and painting operations.

Looking north from Harlem Beach. The Madison Avenue Bridge is behind the woman fishing. In recent years, the rare occasions that
the swing bridges on the Harlem River have opened have usually been to allow cranes to pass. **34**

Looking south on Harlem Beach, a Metro-North New Haven Line train crosses the railroad bridge at Park Avenue. This is the third railroad bridge at

this site since the Harlem River Railroad built the first one here in 1841. The Third Avenue Bridge is visible in the center distance.

View north from the Third Avenue Bridge. The Oak Point Link railroad trestle in the Bronx is to the right and Metro-North's bridge is at center.

Mounds of asphalt and an abandoned concrete plant south of the Third Avenue Bridge. The curved span of the Willis Avenue Bridge is to the far right, next to two flat-topped truss spans on the viaduct of the New York Connecting Railroad Bridge.

Pools of water collect around the salt stored on the ground north of the Triborough Bridge. The bridge's lift span is raised monthly for testing and maintenance purposes but only about three times a year for large ships or cranes on barges.

The Triborough Bridge Authority built the waterfront esplanade and FDR Drive between 125th Street and 92nd Street in 1936.
The pedestrian bridge between 103rd Street and Ward's Island, visible in the distance, was built in 1951 by the authority (by then called the Triborough Bridge and Tunnel Authority). Both the esplanade and bridge were transferred to the City after completion.

Ward's Island hospital buildings are visible from a recreation pier at 107th Street. **40**

At 90th Street, the highway passes a former fire boat pier and environmental center, now used as a ferry landing, before disappearing under Carl Schurz Park. The original name of this part of the highway, East River Drive, is visible on the portal leading under the park.

CHAPTER FOUR

CARL SCHURZ PARK TO THE UNITED NATIONS

The water's edge often seems elusive on the East Side between 90th Street and 42nd Street. Experienced from a car, this is where the FDR Drive passes in and out of several tunnels. Unlike the waterfront on the West Side of Manhattan, which had been pushed out into the Hudson with landfill for real estate development, parks and highways, the East Side's waterfront was limited by the narrowness of the Harlem and East Rivers. The channel between Manhattan and Roosevelt Island, in the East River between about 86th Street to 48th Street, is particularly narrow. Here, it was necessary to squeeze the FDR Drive between expensive residential districts and a bulkhead line so close to the water's edge that two sections of the roadway were built with southbound lanes over northbound lanes. One of these sections, between about 90th Street and 81st Street, is under an esplanade called John Finley Walk, at Carl Schurz Park, which was created when the highway was built. (Carl Schurz Park is also the location of Gracie Mansion, the Mayor's official residence.) The distant views from the high vantage point of John Finley Walk are spectacular but there is little to delight the eye looking down where the water laps against the double-decked roadway. The FDR Drive's second double-decked section is in the East 50s. Instead of an esplanade, public access here is at tiny parks on the highway's roof at the ends of crosstown streets. Between these public areas, collectively called Sutton Place Park, private gardens of townhouses and apartment buildings occupy the roadway's roof, hidden behind high walls.

In the East 60s and 70s the FDR Drive runs uncovered in a straight line, its side-by-side lanes separated from the water by an esplanade. This part of town almost became a major park. Legislation had been passed in 1853 enabling the City to purchase land for Central Park, in the middle of the island, and 160 forested acres known as Jones Wood, between the East River, Third Avenue, 66th Street and 75th Street, for a waterfront park. The provision for Jones Wood was repealed in 1854, however, because powerful business interests in the City wanted the waterfront reserved for commercial use. Since the 1930's this area has been the location of ever-expanding medical complexes. The Hospital for Special Surgery, New York Hospital and Rockefeller University have recently constructed new facilities over the FDR Drive between 72nd Street and 62nd Streets, in accordance with an agreement made with the City in 1973. The waterfront esplanade was reconstructed along the outer edges of these buildings.

At about 60th Street, the esplanade continues on a former highway ramp between the FDR Drive and York Avenue. Just before reaching the Queensboro Bridge, which crosses the river at 59th Street, the ramp veers away from the water, passing Pavilion Park, built on the roof of a former Department of Sanitation facility in 1994. The shoreline under the bridge is inaccessible and desolate. For the half mile or so south of the Queensboro Bridge, only the fragmented Sutton Place Park, at the ends of crosstown streets over the double-decked highway, provides views of the river.

The FDR Drive continues with its lanes side by side and uncovered between 54th Street and 48th Street, at a lower elevation than upland city streets. At the end of 51st Street, a retaining wall has a stairway leading down to Peter Detmold Park, located between the wall and the FDR Drive from 49th to 52nd Streets. There are always plenty of dogs and people in this park who come to use its fenced-in area for dogs to run around in. An elevated walkway, extending out from the retaining wall's stairway, passes over the park and leads to a small esplanade at the water's edge.

The United Nations Headquarters, on the waterfront between 48th Street and 42nd Street, replaced a slaughterhouse district in 1952. The complex was designed by an international team of architects that included Le Corbusier, Oscar Niemeyer and Wallace K. Harrison. Its esplanade, built over the FDR Drive, is generally open during the daytime to the public. To reach it, it is necessary to walk over to First Avenue and enter through a gate at 46th Street.

Carl Schurz Park and John Finley Walk over the FDR Drive. Carl Schurz (1829-1906) was a statesman, the editor of the *Evening Post* and a writer for *Harper's Weekly*. John H. Finley (1863-1940), known for his walks around the city's waterfront, was an editor of *The New York Times* and President of City College.

An iron gate marks the end of Carl Schurz Park at 84th Street, but John Finley Walk continues over the FDR Drive to 81st Street, passing in front of apartment buildings and the private Brearley School, which has a fenced-in play platform extending over the walkway, visible to the right of center. **44**

At 81st Street, stairs descend from the end of John Finley Walk to an esplanade that continues alongside the FDR Drive to 62nd Street.

At the upper left, the Queensboro Bridge passes behind clusters of residential buildings on Roosevelt Island.

The esplanade around the Hospital for Special Surgery seen from a footbridge over the FDR Drive at 71st Street. The FDR Drive is behind the columns facing the esplanade.

View from Roosevelt Island of New York Hospital's twelve-story building and the nearly completed seven-story Hospital for Special Surgery facility under construction over the FDR Drive between 68th and 71st Streets in 1995.

A former highway ramp from York Avenue provides access to Pavilion Park on top of a former Department of Sanitation facility. Alice Aycock's *East River Roundabout* sculpture on the park's roof resembles a roller coaster. A heliport is visible below the park.

A public area at the end of 58th Street at Riverview Terrace. The Queensboro Bridge, which passes over Roosevelt Island and ends in Long Island City in Queens, opened in 1909. A Tramway car to Roosevelt Island is visible below the bridge's roadway.

The park at the end of 57th Street is the largest of the group of small parks found at the dead end streets in the East 50's and collectively called Sutton Place Park. **50**

51   From Roosevelt Island, vines from Sutton Place Park at the end of 57th Street are seen draped over the double-decked FDR Drive.

At 51st Street, a walkway over Peter Detmold Park and the FDR Drive leads to an esplanade at the water's edge between 54th and 51st Streets. The park was named for a local community leader.

53   A private garden overlooking the FDR Drive at about 50th Street.

The FDR Drive south of 51st Street. **54**

Looking south from the esplanade of the United Nations Headquarters.

CHAPTER FIVE

THE UNITED NATIONS TO THE MANHATTAN BRIDGE

The FDR Drive between 92nd Street and Jackson Street on the Lower East Side was completed just before the United States entered World War II. Back then, the waterfront near 34th Street was sometimes called Bristol Basin because landfill for the roadway included rubble from bombed cities in England. The rubble had been ballast for returning supply convoys. Now, large areas of this formerly industrial waterfront are becoming accessible and linked together with esplanades.

The 41st Street Waterside Con Edison plant and its employee parking lot under the FDR Drive block the waterfront, but a landscaped esplanade between 38th and 36th Streets was built in recent years by a developer of a nearby apartment building. South of 36th Street, I had some difficulty determining the path of a public walkway that winds through parking lots, past a Con Edison fuel pier and a landing for ferries to Queens. Where a recently closed heliport blocks the waterfront at 34th Street, the walkway continues under the elevated FDR Drive. Between 33rd and 29th Streets, a landscaped boardwalk and esplanade are maintained by the Water Club, a restaurant on a barge moored at 32nd Street.

Waterside Plaza is a massive complex of four residential towers, each 40 stories high, on a platform in the East River between 29th and 25th Streets. Its lower floors form a solid, four-block-long, six-story-high wall facing the FDR Drive. A narrow walkway, around refuse containers and parked cars between the complex and the FDR Drive, connects to stairs, escalators and ramps leading to Waterside Plaza's public areas with views of the water. A pedestrian bridge over the FDR Drive at 25th Street also leads to these areas. The private United Nations School, on the same platform, is off limits to the public.

Between Waterside Plaza and 18th Street, a marina, gas station, parking garage and parking lots are on a section of shoreline edged by an elevated section of the FDR Drive. This area, called Stuyvesant Cove, is about to become a park with a sandy beach, shade trees, an environmental center, a cafe and recreational barges. A former plan, defeated in 1990, was for a huge mixed-use waterfront development on a platform known as River Walk. While I was photographing for this book, part of this waterfront

was a rubble-strewn staging area for the rehabilitation of the FDR Drive, but it still attracted sunbathers. Just across the roadway are the 56 plain brick buildings of Peter Cooper Village and Stuyvesant Town, which were built in the 1940's by the Metropolitan Life Insurance Company with government subsidies as middle-class, rent-stabilized housing. At the southern end of Stuyvesant Cove near 17th Street, the roadway comes so close to the river's edge that the waterfront is blocked. The 14th Street Con Edison plant and other utilities continue to block the waterfront to 12th Street.

In the mid 19th century, the waterfront of the Lower East Side was a center for building wooden ships, but by the 1880's these vessels were obsolete and the shoreline was the dilapidated border of a notorious slum. The FDR Drive and the 55-acre East River Park, between 12th Street and Jackson Street, smoothed out this formerly irregular shoreline with landfill when they were completed in 1941. At the same time, construction began on massive low-income housing projects near the park that were designed to replace the area's slums. Walkways over the FDR Drive, which runs at ground level for the length of the park, connect the park to 10th Street, 6th Street, Houston Street, Delancey Street and Corlears Hook Park near its southern end.

The Williamsburg Bridge to Brooklyn crosses over the park at Delancey Street. Completed in 1903, it was the second suspension bridge between Brooklyn and Manhattan. The first was the 1883 Brooklyn Bridge, which the Williamsburg Bridge surpassed for a time as the world's longest suspension span. The park's waterfront esplanade passes under the bridge and then follows the shoreline's large curve to the right. Rounding the curve, the Manhattan and Brooklyn Bridges, the Lower Manhattan skyline and the tiny, distant Statue of Liberty come into view.

Immediately south of East River Park, Piers 42-36 occupy a single platform extending from Jackson Street to Jefferson Street. The piers house a cargo shipping company and parking facilities. The southern end of the platform is only about two blocks from the Manhattan Bridge. That bridge, completed in 1909, was the third suspension span between Manhattan and Brooklyn.

Esplanade at 37th Street.

Jet skiers near 33rd Street. Hunter's Point, Queens, is in the background. The tall building at center houses Citicorp's offices in Long Island City. **58**

View south from a Hunter's Point ferry boat. To the right, the FDR Drive descends to ground level behind the 34th Street Heliport. Bellevue and New York University Hospitals buildings are visible behind the FDR Drive. Waterside Plaza, at center, dwarfs the white United Nations School behind it. The 14th Street Con Edison plant and the Williamsburg Bridge are at left center. The Water Club's barge is in front of Waterside Plaza.

View north from 33rd Street. The Queensboro Bridge is at right. The United Nations and a Con Edison smoke stack are at center.
Residential buildings are to the left, and the 34th Street Heliport is in the left foreground. **60**

Waterside Plaza from 30th Street. Davis, Brody & Associates, who designed this 1974 complex, also designed the very similar looking River Park Towers on the Bronx shoreline visible in the view of the railyard at 207th Street in Inwood, on page 22.

Sunbathers at Stuyvesant Cove near 20th Street.   **62**

63   View south of Stuyvesant Cove from the roof of the parking garage at 23rd Street.

View of the 14th Street Con Edison plant from the water. The Empire State Building is in the right distance. **64**

East River Park esplanade. In 1996, tarpaulins covered the Williamsburg Bridge's towers to contain lead paint residue produced during cable repairs, abrasive blasting and painting.

A cyclist on the esplanade is barely visible through an opening in the stage of the crumbling East River Park Amphitheater.
Joseph Papp's free Shakespeare productions were performed here in 1956 before moving to Central Park. **66**

67   Looking north at the Manhattan tower of the Williamsburg Bridge from East River Park.

From the southern end of East River Park, the Statue of Liberty is visible under the Manhattan and Brooklyn Bridges. Lower Manhattan skyscrapers are partly obscured by the shed for piers 36 and 42.

69   The Brooklyn tower of the Manhattan Bridge from the water.

CHAPTER SIX

SOUTH STREET TO SOUTH FERRY

The roadway of the Brooklyn Bridge passes high over South Street at the beginning of the Lower Manhattan shoreline. Its cables, radiating between the tops of its bold stone towers and the roadway, intersect with vertical wires to create a delicate pattern resembling a complex stringed instrument. The strong, Gothic-detailed towers dominated the country's greatest port when the bridge opened in 1883 but, unlike the thriving piers that lined South Street, the bridge never became obsolete.

Colonial New Amsterdam was located on the southern tip of Manhattan south of today's Wall Street. It faced the East River, which was protected from the westerly winds and floating ice that made the Hudson more hazardous for navigation. The shoreline was where Pearl Street is today, three blocks inland from South Street, and the island's southern tip was near where Water and State Streets now meet. Wall Street took its name from the stockade that settlers built in 1635 to protect the village from Indians to the north. As the settlement grew into a port city, the East River shoreline was extended with landfill until South Street was laid out in about 1800. By the mid 19th century, New York had become the busiest port in the country, and South Street was its heart.

South Street's dominance declined after the 1880's when steamships surpassed sailing vessels. The large new transatlantic ships required the open space and deeper waters of the Hudson River. However, ships for coastal and South American trade, and railroad and sanitation barges, docked at piers that still lined the East River shoreline between the Battery and East River Park until the early 1960's. Fishing boats docked at the Fulton Fish Market's Pier 17 until trucks took over in the 1970's. As Manhattan's port activity declined, South Street's piers began disappearing, while urban renewal programs dictated the destruction of nearby 18th- and 19th-century commercial buildings.

To prevent the loss of the last remaining historic structures around South Street, a citizens group obtained landmark status for the area in 1967 and established the South Street Seaport District and South Street Seaport Museum. In 1970, the museum obtained the three-masted cargo ship *Wavertree* and the schooner

Pioneer, both dating from 1885. Five years later, the *Peking,* a four-masted cargo ship dating from 1911, was moored next to the *Wavertree* at Pier 16, and several other ships have since been added to the museum's collection. A large shopping pavilion, built on Pier 17 in 1985, put tourist shops where fishing boats once came. The Fulton Fish Market still operates out of a building next to the north side of the pier and in nearby buildings across South Street. In warm weather, the smells of fish and scented soaps and candles mingle.

Huge, boxy skyscrapers and the elevated FDR Drive seem to push against the historic district and the narrow waterfront walkway leading to the southern tip of Manhattan. At the foot of Wall Street, tennis courts in quilted bubbles are found on Piers 14 and 13. Airport and commuter ferries are among the vessels that come to Piers 11 and 9. The FDR Drive descends to the ground near Pier 6, the location of the Downtown Heliport and the last pier before the ferry terminals at the tip of the island.

The Battery Maritime Building, between Broad and Whitehall Streets, was built in 1909 as one of dozens of ferry terminals that carried over half a million passengers daily to and from Manhattan in the early part of the century. In more recent years, it was the terminal for ferries to Governor's Island, half a mile off the tip of Manhattan. The island had been the location of the colonial governor's official residence and, since the Revolution, a military post. The island's long military history came to an end in 1997 when the Coast Guard base, on the island since 1966, was closed. Now, the future of the island and ferry terminal are undecided.

Next to the Battery Maritime Building is the Staten Island Ferry Terminal. Temporary improvements were made to this bland 1950's building after a fire in 1991. The following year, a competition was held for the design of a new terminal. The winning design, by architects Venturi Scott Brown & Anderson/Schwarz, featured an illuminated clock 120 feet in diameter, facing the harbor and Staten Island. After protests, particularly from Staten Islanders, this design was rejected and a simpler, more conventional design by Anderson/Schwarz is expected to be completed in 2003.

The Brooklyn and Manhattan Bridges seen from the end of Peck Slip mark the beginning of Lower Manhattan.

View south from the end of Catherine Slip. The FDR Drive, completed over South Street in 1954, was elevated to accommodate commercial waterfront activity. South Street Seaport's shopping pavilion on Pier 17 is to the right of the Brooklyn Bridge tower. The white building immediately to the right of Pier 17 is part of the Fulton Fish Market.

The Fulton Fish Market. Most business is conducted at this wholesale market between midnight and about 9 A.M.
A corner of the shopping pavilion at Pier 17 is visible under the FDR Drive viaduct to the right.

An entry in the New York City Corvette Club's Second Annual Corvette Show on the north side of
Pier 17, June 2, 1996. The Brooklyn Bridge is behind it. **74**

The *Peking* at South Street Seaport's Pier 16.

The South Street Seaport on the Fourth of July, 1995. Some of the office towers in the background were built with air rights transferred from buildings in the South Street Seaport Historic District.

View north from Pier 16 of Pier 17 and the Brooklyn and Manhattan Bridges. Between 1814 and 1924, the Fulton Ferry to Brooklyn departed from terminals located here.

Lower Manhattan from the Brooklyn Heights Esplanade. The Downtown Heliport's striped building on Pier 6 is at the base of One New York Plaza, the southernmost office building in the photo. The Battery Maritime Building's three arched portals and the square portals of the Staten Island Ferry Terminal are at the island's tip. To the left, the four towers of the Main Building at Ellis Island are visible against the New Jersey horizon. The roof of Pier 3 in Brooklyn is in the foreground.

A Governor's Island ferry is in one of the Battery Maritime Building's slips. The gridlike facade behind it at left is One New York Plaza. At right, office
buildings recede up Broad Street.

The Staten Island Ferry Terminal in 1996. The temporary ribbed metal facade replaced the original 1954 exterior after a fire in 1991.

The *Governor Herbert H. Lehman* in a slip at the Staten Island Ferry Terminal.

CHAPTER SEVEN

BATTERY PARK
AND BATTERY
PARK CITY

There is green space near the water at Battery Park and the waterfront highway has disappeared into a tunnel. The view from here is of the wide-open Upper New York Bay, with the Statue of Liberty and Ellis Island in the distance. The waterfront esplanade follows the curve of the southern tip of the island, leading from its East Side to its West Side.

Three million tourists come to Battery Park each year for the expansive view and to board ferries to the Statue of Liberty and Ellis Island. The park's name comes from artillery installations that have stood at the tip of the island since early colonial times. The original fortifications have disappeared, but Castle Clinton National Monument, a circular fort constructed in 1811 in preparation for the War of 1812, still stands. Originally called the West Battery, the fort was built on its own tiny island, reached by a causeway, about 300 feet off Manhattan's shore. Castle William, built on Governor's Island in 1811, was the East Battery. No guns were ever fired in wartime from either fort, and Castle Clinton was ceded to the City in 1823. In the years from 1824 to 1855 it was an entertainment hall called Castle Garden, where P. T. Barnum presented soprano Jenny Lind, known as the Swedish Nightingale, in 1850. It became the Emigrant Landing Depot between 1855 and 1890, preceding Ellis Island in this function; and, between 1896 and 1941, the location of the New York Aquarium. By 1872, Battery Park had been extended with landfill and Castle Clinton was no longer on a separate island. Today, tickets for the ferries to the Statue of Liberty and Ellis Island are sold in Castle Clinton's courtyard.

Several war memorials are located in the park, including the East Coast Memorial honoring servicemen lost in the Atlantic during World War II and the Merchant Mariners Memorial. In 1919, a World War I memorial clock was placed in the tower of Pier A at the west end of the park.

Battery Park almost became the site of approach ramps for a major suspension bridge that was planned between the lower tip of Manhattan and Brooklyn in the late 1930's. Sentiment in Manhattan was largely against the bridge because the park and Castle Clinton would be destroyed and the famous downtown skyline would be dominated by the bridge's huge Manhattan tower and anchorage. The bridge was a proposal of Robert Moses, who headed several state and city agencies at the time, including the Triborough Bridge Authority and the Department of Parks, and who exercised a vast influence over New York's public works construction for over three decades. The bridge would probably have been built if it hadn't been vetoed by Secretary of War Harry Woodring in 1939. President Franklin D. Roosevelt, who had previously been Governor of New York and disliked both the bridge plan and Robert Moses, was reputedly behind the veto. The Brooklyn-Battery Tunnel, built instead, is hidden under the park. Other tunnels under the park are the roadway connecting the FDR Drive to West Street, the loop at the end of the Nos. 1 and 9 IRT subway lines and a tunnel for the Nos. 4 and 5 IRT lines. In 1996, a major restoration of the 23-acre park began with structural repairs and work on the park's sea wall and promenade which will connect to the esplanade of Battery Park City that begins at the western edge of the park.

Battery Park City is on 92 acres of landfill that extend out into the Hudson River. The landfill, partly from the excavation for the World Trade Center, buried the foundations of about seventeen piers. On this newest extension of Manhattan, residential buildings and the massive World Financial Center face a landscape of lush lawns and gardens bordered by an esplanade at the water's edge. Thirty percent of the development is reserved for open public space, but hardly a speck of litter or patch of worn lawn can be found. Battery Park City Authority, established by the State in 1968, financed the landfill, infrastructure and public areas by issuing State bonds and chose a commercial developer to develop the commercial and residential areas. Construction began in 1974 at Gateway Plaza, a residential complex off Liberty Street. Now, about 7,500 people live in Battery Park City's 18 residential buildings and over 20,000 work in its office buildings. When the last buildings are completed, it is expected that 25,000 people will reside and 35,000 will work here.

West Street separates Battery Park City from the rest of Manhattan. Two enclosed pedestrian bridges cross over West Street to the World Financial Center. At Chambers Street, the Tribeca Bridge over West Street carries pedestrians to Stuyvesant High School and the northern end of Battery Park City.

Ferries to Liberty and Ellis Islands board at Battery Park. The Statue of Liberty is at the far right.

The Battery Park esplanade.

Ferry tickets are sold within the red sandstone walls of Castle Clinton. Outside, hot dogs and souvenirs are sold from carts. The 1811 fort was designed by John McComb, Jr. The following year, City Hall, which McComb designed with Joseph François Mangin, was completed.

The eagle by Albino Manca and eight granite slabs inscribed with the names of the 4,596 service men who died in the Atlantic during World War II form the East Coast Memorial, dedicated by President John F. Kennedy in 1963. The reflective building is 17 State Street.

The sculptor Marisol based the 1991 American Merchant Mariners' Memorial on a photograph taken by a U-boat skipper of American Merchant Mariners on a raft after their boat was sunk in an attack. The men died at sea. At high tide, the head of the figure in the water is submerged. To the right, a World War I memorial clock is in the tower of Pier A, parts of which date from 1885. The four-towered Main Building at Ellis Island is on the left horizon.

A structure with a viewing platform on its roof and a restaurant in its right arch at Robert F. Wagner, Jr. Park. The park, designed by landscape architects Hannah/Olin and garden designer Lynden B. Miller, opened at the southern end of Battery Park City in 1996.

The open space under the viewing platform frames a ferry heading to the Statue of Liberty. The structure was designed by architects Rodolfo Machado and Jorge Silvetti.

A bench on top of the viewing platform. The stepped pyramidlike roof belongs to the Museum of Jewish Heritage—A Living Memorial to the Holocaust, designed by Kevin Roche and opened in 1997. To the right are residential buildings at Battery Park City. Jersey City, across the Hudson, is to the left. **90**

The esplanade at South Cove. The South and North Coves are two indentations in Battery Park City's otherwise straight waterfront edge.

Battery Park City's World Financial Center, designed by Cesar Pelli, is the backdrop of the marina at North Cove.   **92**

93   A ferry from New Jersey approaches the World Financial Center. Jersey City is in the distance.

A lawn in Rockefeller Park near Battery Park City's north end.

Fishing on the Battery Park City esplanade.

Sunbathers at Rockefeller Park.

Stuyvesant High School and Rockefeller Park, at the squared-off northern end of Battery Park City near Chambers Street, are at center. West Street and the beginning of the temporary asphalt esplanade of Hudson River Park are near the water's edge at the bottom.

CHAPTER EIGHT

CHAMBERS STREET TO WEST 23RD STREET

An asphalt strip beginning slightly north of Chambers Street is gradually being built through the narrow space between the waterfront roadway and the waterfront itself. For now, it is an interim walkway and bikeway but eventually it is to become a landscaped waterfront park and esplanade, called Hudson River Park. It will extend to 59th Street and open out onto several of the remaining piers that are no longer used for maritime purposes.

Almost all traces of the once crowded and intensely commercial waterfront of Tribeca, the West Village and Chelsea have been swept away over the past two decades. In the early 1900's, when New York was one of the busiest ports in the world, this part of the waterfront was teeming with cargo, longshoremen and horse-drawn vehicles along a nearly solid wall of piers. Passengers crowded into ocean liner piers and ferry terminals. Freight rail cars clustered around float bridges that they rolled over to get on to special barges with tracks called car floats. Trains had run in the streets of Manhattan's West Side ever since the Hudson River Railroad laid its tracks between Canal Street and Spuyten Duyvil in 1847. North of 60th Street the tracks run along the Hudson shoreline, but in this part of town they were laid down 10th and 11th Avenues and other nearby streets. Well into the 1930's, locomotives of the New York Central Railroad (successor to the Hudson River Railroad) still pulled freight trains in the streets, following slowly behind "West Side cowboys," men on horseback carrying red flags.

The world's longest and most fashionable ocean liners once came to the 800-foot Chelsea Piers whose elegant facades extended between Little West 12th Street and 22nd Street. The Cunard Line's 787-foot *Lusitania* and 790-foot *Mauritania,* each launched in 1907, came to these piers. The War Department, which controlled the pierhead line, would not permit these piers to extend far enough out to accommodate these ocean liners because the Hudson is relatively narrow at this point. Instead, the waterfront was excavated back from 13th Avenue, to allow for the 800-foot length. Even longer ships made the Chelsea Piers obsolete almost immediately, however. The White Star Line's *Titanic,* scheduled to arrive at Chelsea Pier 54 on its 1912 maiden voyage, was 882 feet long. After 1935, when ocean liners exceeding 1,000 feet in length began using longer piers in the West 40s, the Chelsea Piers came to be used mostly as cargo terminals.

Automobile traffic increased the chaos around West Street, particularly after the Holland Tunnel to New Jersey opened near Canal Street in 1927. The elevated Miller Highway, named after its promoter, Manhattan Borough President Julius Miller, but almost always known as the West Side Highway, was built along the waterfront between Rector Street and 72nd Street to separate automobile traffic from rail and pier traffic. Mostly completed by 1931, the elevated roadway was part of a program called the West Side Improvement, which also moved the New York Central tracks from the streets to a new elevated rail line between Canal Street and the 30th Street railyard and then into an open cut between the railyard and 60th Street by 1934. The Henry Hudson Parkway, beginning north of 72nd Street, was also part of the West Side Improvement.

By the 1970's, the condition of the neglected but busy West Side Highway matched the decay of the little-used piers. After part of the roadway collapsed under a loaded dump truck near Gansevoort Street in 1973, it was demolished in stages south of 59th Street between 1976 and 1989. At the same time, many piers were reduced to rotting platforms in the water. A block or so inland, the southern end of the elevated rail line disappeared.

Government and civic leaders proposed a plan in the early 1970's to restore the Hudson River waterfront from the Battery to 42nd Street with landfill and a buried interstate highway. The plan, which came to be called Westway, was killed in the 1980s after numerous delays and quarrels over environmental issues. The waterfront gradually became a rubble-strewn open space.

Now, Hudson River Park is being planned by the Hudson River Park Conservancy, a subsidiary of the New York State Urban Development Corporation. No landfill will extend this modest waterfront park, which is required to be financially self-supporting. The Conservancy promises that no residential, hotel or office buildings will be built on the park's designated commercial areas. Instead, there will be concessions for sports, restaurants and maritime-related businesses. Local communities, suspicious that commercial interests will take over the park, are participating in the park's design with the master design team, Quennell Rothschild Associates/Signe Nielson.

99   The gate at Pier 25, the first pier north of Battery Park City.

Pier 25, left of center, has sandy volleyball courts, a miniature golf course, a cafe, an old tug boat and a turn-of-the-century ferry boat called the *Yankee*. A contemporary ferry heads south to Battery Park City. Part of Pier 26 is to the right. Near the bottom, a white barrier separates a row of parked cars from Hudson River Park's asphalt esplanade.

Beyond the volleyball players and the *Yankee* on Pier 25, the shedlike structures for the Hudson River Project and Downtown Boathouse are visible on Pier 26. The Hudson River Project is devoted to the protection and restoration of the Hudson River Estuary environment. The Downtown Boathouse is a volunteer organization of kayakers, canoers and rowboaters.

A ventilation building for the Holland Tunnel stands in the water off of Canal Street. In 1996 a pair of finger piers, called Pier 34, were built as escape routes from the tunnel. Pier 34's southern "finger" is open to the public. The decaying Pier 32, to the south of Pier 34, is one of several rotted piers designated to become wildlife refuges.

103   The public area on Pier 34, one of thirteen of Hudson River Park's piers that are reserved for recreation.

There are 2,000 parking spaces on Pier 40, designated as a site for a mix of recreational and commercial development.
Built in 1962, it extends three blocks from King Street to Leroy Street. **104**

A baseball field will be built on part of Pier 40's roof, and an indoor soccer field and neighborhood recreation center will be built on its lower levels in 1998. Together, these recreation areas will occupy about 10% of the pier; the rest will remain parking space for at least three years.

View north from Pier 40. Trees and landscaping surround the Morton Street ventilation structure and escape shafts for tunnels that carry PATH (Port Authority Trans Hudson) trains between Manhattan and New Jersey. Route 9A, which includes West Street, to the right, is being reconstructed as a tree-lined boulevard.

107   View south from Pier 45, near Christopher Street. Two barges are moored at the end of Pier 40.

The north side of Pier 45.

An evening performance of opera and show tunes on Pier 45.

The smoke stacks at center, on Gansevoort Peninsula, are part of the Gansevoort Destructor Plant, an abandoned refuse incinerator. An abandoned Department of Sanitation marine transfer station is to the far left. A vestigial portion of 13th Avenue, once at this part of the waterfront, remains at the end of the peninsula. **110**

111   A salt storage shed on Gansevoort Peninsula. The peninsula is designated to become a recreation area for Hudson River Park.

The fireboat *John D. McKean* at Pier 53 on the north side of Gansevoort Peninsula.

View from the *John D. McKean's* crow's nest. The firehouse sign says Company 2 but it is occupied by Company 1, Manhattan's last active fireboat company on the Hudson. Pier 54, of the old Chelsea Piers, to the far left, was where the *Titanic* was scheduled to arrive on its maiden voyage in 1912.

Looking south, the smokestacks on Gansevoort peninsula rise above the skeleton of Pier 54's facade, which was left when the pier was demolished in 1991. Concrete barriers and chain link fencing divide the temporary esplanade from West Street.

The Chelsea Piers Sports and Entertainment Complex occupies Piers 59, 60, 61 and 62 between 17th and 22nd Streets. This section of the 1910 Chelsea Piers, remodeled with utilitarian exteriors in 1963, is one of Hudson River Park's sites designated for commercial development.

Looking south from the marina docks at Pier 59 a week after they were completed in 1996. Pier 57, in the distance, was built in 1954 and is used as a bus garage. A crowd of pilings alongside Pier 57 is all that remains of Pier 58. **116**

The *Frying Pan,* an old lighthouse ship, is on display in front of Pier 61, which houses two year-round ice-skating rinks.

A public esplanade borders the outer edges of all the piers at the complex, including the golf driving range enclosed in a huge net structure on Pier 60. In the foreground is a dealer's display of yachts between Piers 59 and 60.

119   Pier 62 has fenced-off areas for skating and skateboarding. The white bubble is on top of Pier 63 where the Chelsea Equestrian Center is located.

CHAPTER NINE

WEST 23RD
STREET TO
RIVERSIDE PARK

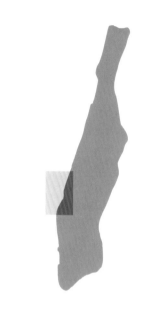

North of 23rd Street, a few relics of the freight railroads that once ran on the West Side survive. A wooden float bridge, still in the water off 26th Street, was built in 1954 by the Baltimore and Ohio (B & O) Railroad. Freight railroad cars rolled over the float bridge's tracks to move from car floats to tracks under the West Side Highway that led to a B & O warehouse across 12th Avenue. The float bridge was last used in 1973, and the warehouse is now occupied by a mini-storage company. A few blocks to the north, on the east side of 12th Avenue, part of the 1934 elevated rail line built by the New York Central Railroad descends to ground level between 30th and 33rd Streets, at the edge of a railyard now occupied by the Long Island Rail Road. From here, the tracks continue north in a cut between 10th and 11th Avenues until they reach the former New York Central railyard at 60th Street. The elevated line has not been used in years, but the tracks in the cut are used today by Amtrak Passenger Service running out of Penn Station.

A heliport and a pound for towed cars on Pier 76 block the esplanade between 30th and 37th Street but public access to the waterfront begins again near 37th Street, at Pier 78, owned by New York Waterway, which operates several Hudson River ferries. The company is planning to build a larger terminal in the space around a ventilation building of the Lincoln Tunnel one block north at Pier 79.

At 41st Street the waterfront abruptly becomes a crowded tourist area with the atmosphere of a chaotic parking lot. Pier 81, off 41st Street, is used by World Yacht dinner cruise and touring boats. Circle Line touring boats that go all the way around Manhattan leave from Pier 83, between 42nd and 43rd Streets. At Pier 86, the World War II aircraft carrier USS *Intrepid* dominates the Intrepid Sea Air & Space Museum off 46th Street. Hudson River Park's landscaped esplanade will eventually continue through this busy area, and end at 59th Street.

The longest transatlantic ocean liners in history berthed at Piers 86, 88, 90 and 92 between 46th and 52nd Streets from the late 1930's to the early 1970's. The United States Line's 990-foot *United States,* commissioned in 1952 as the world's fastest ocean liner, berthed at Pier 86, where the *Intrepid* is today. The French Line's elegant 1,028-foot *Normandie,* launched in 1935 as the first ship to exceed 1,000 feet, was moored at Pier 88 when it was destroyed by fire while being refitted as a troop ship in 1942. The *France,* launched in 1961, also berthed at Pier 88. At 1,035 feet, it was the longest ocean liner ever. The Cunard Line's 1,018-foot *Queen Mary* of 1936 and the 1,031-foot *Queen Elizabeth* of 1940 used Pier 90. When Piers 88, 90 and 92 were rebuilt as the present Passenger Ship Terminal in the early 1970's, most transatlantic ocean liners had been superseded by jet airplanes. An exception was Cunard's 963-foot *Queen Elizabeth 2,* whose maiden voyage was in 1969. The *QE2* now shares the Passenger Ship Terminal with cruise ships. The terminal runs at a deficit and its piers are used for trade shows off season.

Twelfth Avenue rises at 59th Street on the only remaining portion of the elevated West Side Highway, which passes over the former 60th Street yard of the New York Central Railroad. Donald Trump took an option in 1974 to buy the site from Penn Central, the railroad's successor. In 1985 he proposed Television City, featuring a 150-story skyscraper, six residential buildings over 70 stories high and a center for motion picture and television studios. Community groups, civic associations and politicians have been debating the scale of the site's development ever since. Television City was replaced by the current Riverside South plan, which calls for 16 residential buildings between 18 and 49 stories high, 1.8 million square feet of commercial development and a 23-acre public waterfront park. While the site was being debated, the heavily used roadway, which was to have been tunneled under the park, had deteriorated to the point that its rehabilitation could not be delayed. The rehabilitation took four years, cost $72 million and left the highway over the planned waterfront park. The State and City now say they can't afford to spend the additional $200 million to rebuild the highway in a tunnel. More debate seems likely.

Construction began on the first two buildings of Riverside South in early 1997. There was time for me to photograph the incomplete towers, but I prefer the images of the site while it was still open and empty, except for the highway. There is nothing else like it left in Manhattan.

A waterside restaurant and landscaped boardwalk appeared at the water's edge near 25th Street in 1996 but disappeared at the end of its 18-month lease. Behind it, the B & O Railroad float bridge extends into the Hudson.

Until 1973, railroad cars rolled on tracks between the wooden trusses of this float bridge to reach tracks on 12th Avenue.

Railroad cars from the float bridge came directly into the B & O Freight Terminal, now occupied by a storage company.
The Starrett-Lehigh Building behind it also had tracks leading into its ground floor. In the foreground, a concrete barrier separates the
asphalt esplanade from 12th Avenue. The metal sphere is a barrier between the bench and skaters and cyclists.

The northern vestigial section of the elevated railroad line, built as part of the West Side Improvement in 1934, passes over the edge of the Long Island Rail Road railyard between 30th and 33rd Streets. **124**

View from the temporary asphalt waterfront esplanade near 26th Street. The open areas of the West 20's had been railyards earlier in the century. The black glass exterior of the Jacob K. Javits Convention Center is in the left distance.

The end of the temporary esplanade at 31st Street. Behind the fence is a heliport. The cut-off end of the elevated rail line is at the far right.

Passengers wait for ferries to New Jersey at Pier 78. To the right, Pier 79 surrounds the base of a ventilation building for the
Lincoln Tunnel, which goes under the Hudson at 39th Street. A new ferry terminal will replace the white shed at the base of Pier 79.
World Yacht touring boats are visible at Pier 81 off 41st Street, and the aircraft carrier USS *Intrepid* is at Pier 86 off 46th Street.

Circle Line touring boats leave from Pier 83 near 42nd Street.

Fighter planes on the USS *Intrepid's* deck.

View of the Passenger Ship Terminal from a ferry boat to New Jersey. The white ship to the right, the *Meridian*, is about to back out from Berth 1 of Pier 88. The *Song of America* is at Berth 2 and the *Island Breeze* is at Berth 3 at Pier 90.

131   Small pleasure boats wait as the *Meridian*, launched as the *Galileo Galilei* in 1963, backs out from the Passenger Ship Terminal.

The *Dreamward*, a cruise ship dating from 1992, at Pier 88.

The *Queen Elizabeth 2* and a workboat at Pier 90.

A sanitation truck near Pier 99 at 59th Street, which has a marine transfer facility at its far end. Beyond the truck,
12th Avenue ascends to become the elevated West Side Highway over the Riverside South site. **134**

The West Side Highway over the Riverside South site, formerly a Penn Central railyard.

As development plans for Riverside South were debated, it began returning to nature. **136**

137   Near 62nd Street is the skeleton of a railyard pier melted by a fire.

At the northern end of the Riverside South, a gantry stands with huge gears and a drawbridge. Like the smaller float bridge off 26th Street, this gantry once aligned with the tracks of car floats so that freight cars could easily roll into land. **138**

139   View south toward the gantry from the southern edge of Riverside Park at 72nd Street.

CHAPTER TEN

RIVERSIDE PARK TO THE GEORGE WASHINGTON BRIDGE

The last segment of this journey, like the first, is mostly through city parkland. Riverside Park is on the shoreline and bluffs facing the Hudson River between 72nd and 125th Streets and again between 135th and 158th Streets. A commercial district, called Manhattanville, is in a gap in the bluffs between the park's two sections. Riverside Drive, which runs along the top of the bluffs, is carried over Manhattanville on a high viaduct. The Henry Hudson Parkway runs through the park and crosses over Manhattanville on a lower viaduct. A third viaduct carries tracks that emerge from a tunnel at 123rd Street and continue above ground through the northern section of the park.

When the Hudson River Railroad laid tracks up Manhattan's shoreline in 1847, they were quickly surrounded by coal yards, dumps and industrial structures. To screen the view from new residential districts being planned on the West Side, the City acquired the land on the bluffs between 72nd and 125th Streets and commissioned Frederick Law Olmsted, Central Park's chief designer, to design Riverside Drive and a park on the bluffs. His plan, presented in 1875, was carried out with revisions by later designers, including Samuel Parsons, Jr., Calvert Vaux and F. Stewart Williamson. By 1910, Riverside Drive and the original, narrow Riverside Park, up to 155th Street, and the lacy viaduct over 125th Street were complete.

After the George Washington Bridge opened in 1931, there was great demand for a new highway down the West Side to keep traffic off Riverside Drive and local streets. To achieve this, the Henry Hudson Parkway and the extension of the park over the tracks were completed in 1937 as part of the West Side Improvement program. The Parkway, between 72nd Street and the City line in the Bronx, was one of several landscaped highways built by the Department of Parks before World War II under the direction of City Parks Commissioner Robert Moses. At the same time, Moses extended Riverside Park, between 72nd and 125th Streets, to its present seawall with 3 million cubic yards of landfill and hid the tracks in a tunnel under the landfill.

In the six decades since the park's expansion, it has matured into a lush, if slightly ragged, environment. Ornamental arches on the parkway's 79th Street traffic circle, arched ventilation openings with ornamental grillwork in walls enclosing the railroad tracks, and arched detailing around playgrounds have come to blend with the neoclassi-

cal and rustic details of the original park to create a dreamily pastoral place, in spite of being one of the most heavily used parks in the city.

Riverside Park north of 135th Street, which was not significantly extended in the 1930's, is cut off from the adjoining neighborhoods by Riverside Drive's high retaining wall, railroad tracks and the Henry Hudson Parkway. It is the location of the North River Wastewater Treatment Plant, on the waterfront between 137th and 145th Streets, which began operating in 1986. The 28-acre Riverbank State Park, which opened on top of the plant in 1993, is connected to Riverside Drive by a bridge at each end. North of the plant, Riverside Park has recently been extended from 155th Street to meet Fort Washington Park at 158th Street, in the shadows of parkway traffic ramps. More traffic ramps between 168th Street and the George Washington Bridge continue to make the park difficult to reach from local streets, although desolate pedestrian overpasses do exist at 175th and 181st Streets.

The Manhattan tower of the George Washington Bridge is on Jeffrey's Hook, a point of land in Fort Washington Park that extends into the Hudson at 178th Street. The bridge, designed by Othmar Hermann Ammann, was the longest suspension bridge in the world when it opened. Its steel towers were originally to be hidden in a granite exterior designed by the architect Cass Gilbert but money ran out and the towers remain uncovered. Next to the bridge's tower is the Little Red Lighthouse, made famous as the subject of Hildegarde Hoyt Swift and Lynd Ward's 1942 book, *The Little Red Lighthouse and the Great Gray Bridge.* The U.S. Coast Guard brought the 1880 lighthouse from Sandy Hook, New Jersey, in 1921, but the bridge made it obsolete ten years later. When the Coast Guard announced plans to auction the lighthouse in 1947, a barrage of letters and coins sent by children who had read the book saved it. The lighthouse was turned over to the Parks Department in 1951 and designated a city landmark in 1991.

I have almost come full cycle. North of the bridge's tower, the waterfront is blocked by railroad tracks. So, as I began my journey with a hairpin turn, I turn again, following a path and a neglected walkway over the tracks and parkway back to Riverside Drive near 181st Street, my old neighborhood.

The Riverside Park Esplanade near 72nd Street. In the distance is the 79th Street Marina. The crane was used for the upgrading of its docks.

The marina faces the 79th Street traffic circle, which surrounds a rotunda where performances are sometimes given. The rotunda's entrance is through the three arches at center.

Riverside Park operates the marina where seventy boat owners live year round and visiting boats can refuel.

View south from an apartment window on Riverside Drive at 86th Street. The parkway runs close to the water's edge at the lower right corner. The Lower Promenade, near the bottom center, is a walkway on the roofed-over railroad tracks. The marina is in the middle distance. The architectural designer and landscape architect for the park's 1937 extension were Clinton F. Loyd and Gilmore D. Clarke, respectively. **144**

145   A kayaker at the north end of the marina. The large structure in the water at center, called a dolphin, protects the marina from ice floes.

A pedestrian tunnel under the Henry Hudson Parkway near 84th Street. The three arches with grillwork screens in the stone wall provide safety exits and air to the railroad tracks enclosed behind it. The park's Lower Promenade is above the wall.

147   The rustic retaining wall supporting Riverside Drive is part of the original Olmsted landscape.

Sledding near 113th Street on the steep incline between Riverside Drive and the parkway, which is visible as a black line at the water's edge. **148**

149   At 125th Street, Riverside Drive passes over Manhattanville on a viaduct supported by lacy steel arches.

The Riverside Drive viaduct was designed by F. Stewart Williamson to be appreciated from the water in an era when ferries came to 125th Street and other passenger boats passed nearby. The Henry Hudson Parkway viaduct is in front of it, and the railroad viaduct is hidden between them. **150**

At 135th Street, Riverside Drive continues above a retaining wall with steps leading down to Manhattanville. The small bridge to the left is a walkway between Riverside Drive and Riverbank State Park on the roof of the North River Wastewater Treatment Plant. North River is an old name for the Hudson River. The Delaware River was the South River.

View south from Riverbank State Park of the Department of Sanitation marine transfer station at 135th Street.
The barge of refuse will be towed to the Fresh Kills Landfill waste disposal facility on Staten Island.

The North River Wastewater Treatment Plant treats wastewater from Manhattan's West Side between Bank Street in Greenwich Village and Manhattan's northern tip. On its roof, picnic areas, sports facilities and chimneys are part of the landscape of Riverbank State Park, designed by Richard Dattner.

The sludge boat *Newtown Creek* transports sludge from the North River plant to a dewatering facility on Ward's Island.
After dewatering, some of the sludge is further processed into fertilizers or soil enhancers that are sold around the country.
The rest of the dewatered sludge is sent to landfill waste disposal locations.

View north towards the George Washington Bridge from Riverbank State Park.

Fishing in Riverside Park near 152nd Street. Among the many kinds of fish caught in the waters around Manhattan are striped bass, summer and winter flounder, porgies, weakfish, bluefish, monkfish and tautogs.

View from Hood Wright Park at 175th Street and Haven Avenue. A walkway to Fort Washington Park, at lower right, is enclosed in chain link fencing. The tarpaulin on the George Washington Bridge contains an area being blasted and painted.

The Little Red Lighthouse and the George Washington Bridge.   **158**